Contents

Heroes and villains

People love to hear about heroes and villains.

Heroes

Heroes are people who have done something brave or good.

People often admire heroes.

HEROES
AND VILLAINS

Alison Hawes

Editorial consultants: Cliff Moon,
Lorraine Petersen and Frances Ridley

Pleas

Helping Everyone Achieve

nasen
NASEN House, 4/5 Amber Business Village, Amber Close,
Amington, Tamworth, Staffordshire B77 4RP

Rising Stars UK Ltd.
22 Grafton Street, London W1S 4EX
www.risingstars-uk.com

Every effort has been made to trace copyright holders and obtain their permission for use of copyright material. The publisher will gladly receive information enabling them to rectify any error or omission in subsequent editions.
All facts are correct at time of going to press.

Published 2007

Cover design: Button plc
Cover images: Alamy
Text design and typesetting: Andy Wilson
Publisher: Gill Budgell
Project management and editorial: Lesley Densham
Editing: Deborah Kespert
Editorial consultants: Cliff Moon, Lorraine Petersen and Frances Ridley
Illustrations: Chris King: pages 16–17, 24–25, 36–37, 38–39
Photos: Alamy: pages 8, 18, 21, 27, 30, 33, 34, 40, 42
BBC: page 11 (© BBC Photo Library)
Empics: pages 13, 35, 40
Getty Images: pages 12, 14, 15, 18, 19, 20, 21, 33
Kobal: pages 4–5, 6, 7, 9, 10, 22–23, 26–27, 28, 29, 30, 31, 32, 34, 41, 43

British Library Cataloguing in Publication Data.
A CIP record for this book is available from the British Library.

ISBN: 978-1-84680-193-8

Printed by Craft Print International Limited, Singapore

Villains

Villains are people who have done something cruel or bad.

People don't often admire villains.

Superheroes

Superheroes are **fictional** heroes.
They aren't real. They have superpowers
or super skills to help them be heroes.

Some superheroes wear
flashy costumes, which
hide who they really are.

Spiderman is really
Peter Parker.

Batman is really
Bruce Wayne.

Did you know?

Many superheroes
began their lives in
comic strips.

POW!

Superman was the first comic-book superhero.

He has super hearing.

He has super vision.

He is super strong.

He is bulletproof.

He can freeze things with his breath.

He can fly.

Heroes in books

In a book, the hero is usually the main **character**.

Harry Potter

Harry is a teenage wizard. He faces many dangers but he has his friends and his magic to help him.

DVD fact!

The DVD of 'Harry Potter and the Goblet of Fire' is the fastest-selling DVD of all time.

Alex Rider

Alex is a teenage spy who is made to work for MI6. He has cool gadgets to help him overcome his enemies.

Alex makes a quick getaway on this quad bike.

Did you know?

Alex Rider supports Chelsea football club.

Film and TV heroes

In films and on TV, the hero is often called the 'good guy'.

James Bond

James Bond is a secret agent. In the Bond films, he faces many dangers. He often uses gadgets to help him.

In 'Thunderball', James uses a jet pack to escape.

Bond fact!

James Bond's name comes from the author of a book on birds.

Dr Who

Dr Who is a Time Lord who travels through time and space in a machine called the TARDIS.

The word 'TARDIS' stands for Time And Relative Dimensions In Space.

Dr Who's most famous enemies are the Daleks and the Cybermen.

Did you know?

Dr Who is the longest running **science-fiction** programme in the world. It began in 1963.

POW!

Real-life heroes

Real-life heroes often do something very brave.

Ernest Shackleton

Ernest Shackleton was a ship's captain. In 1916, his ship was travelling in the **Antarctic**. It got crushed by ice and it sank.

Shackleton travelled 800 miles in a lifeboat with five of his men to get help. In the end, the whole crew was rescued.

Some people think Oscar Schindler was a villain who became a hero.

He was a **Nazi** factory owner, who made lots of money during World War II.

Oscar Schindler

In the end, he lost most of this money. He spent it saving his Jewish factory workers. Years later, he met some of the people he saved.

Schindler fact!

Oscar saved over 1,000 workers.

Harriet Tubman lived in the 1800s.
She was a slave in the United States.
When Harriet was in her twenties,
she escaped from her owners.

Harriet Tubman

Harriet helped hundreds
of other slaves to escape.
She is on the left in this
photo with some of the
people she helped.

Did you know?

Between 1650 and
1900, over ten million
Africans were kidnapped
and sold as slaves.

In the early 1900s,
in the UK, men could
vote in elections
but women could not.

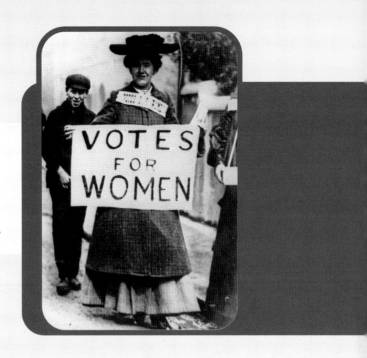

Emmeline Pankhurst

Emmeline Pankhurst
protested against
this law. She was
put in prison and
even went on
hunger strike.

In 1928, the law
was changed.
At last, women
could vote.

Zero to Hero (Part one)

Mrs Wilson lives in the same street as Russ and me.

Mrs Wilson doesn't like us and we don't like her much, either.

She's always getting at us.

She's always yelling at us.

If we play football in the street, she yells, "Mind my car!"

If we skateboard on the pavement, she yells, "Get out of my way!"

If we just hang about having a laugh, she yells, "Keep the noise down!"

Sometimes we just ignore her.

Sometimes we answer back.

But whatever we do, it's wrong.

We just can't win.

Continued on page 24

War heroes

The Victoria Cross is a medal given to the bravest war heroes.

Jack Cornwell

Jack Cornwell was the youngest war hero in World War I. He was a teenager when he won the Victoria Cross.

Jack was a gunner on a warship. He was badly injured in a sea battle but he bravely stayed at his gun post.

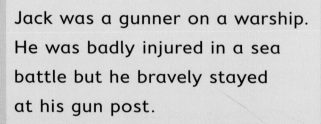

Johnson Beharry

Johnson Beharry was given the Victoria Cross in 2005. He was a soldier in Iraq.

In 2004, he was badly injured in two different **ambushes**. Both times, he saved the lives of the soldiers with him.

Johnson was driving a **Warrior** each time he was ambushed.

Victoria Cross facts!

Since 1856, over 1,000 people have won the Victoria Cross. Only three people have won it twice.

Sporting heroes

Some people's heroes are great sportsmen.

Steve Redgrave

Some people say Steve Redgrave is the greatest sportsman ever.

Steve Redgrave was an Olympic rower. He won five gold medals for rowing in five different Olympic Games. This is a world record.

Did you know?

Steve Redgrave is **diabetic**. This did not stop him from winning all those medals.

POW!

Some people say Pelé is
the greatest footballer ever.

Pelé

Pelé was a famous
footballer from the
1950s to the 1970s.
He played for Brazil
in the World Cup.

Pelé was the youngest person
to score in a World Cup.
He is also the only footballer
to win three World Cups.

Pelé fact!

Pelé's real name is
Edson Arantes do
Nascimento.

Folk heroes

Folk heroes are **characters** in old stories, poems and songs. They are sometimes based on real people who lived long ago.

Robin Hood

Robin Hood is a folk hero. The stories about him may not be true but he may have been a real person.

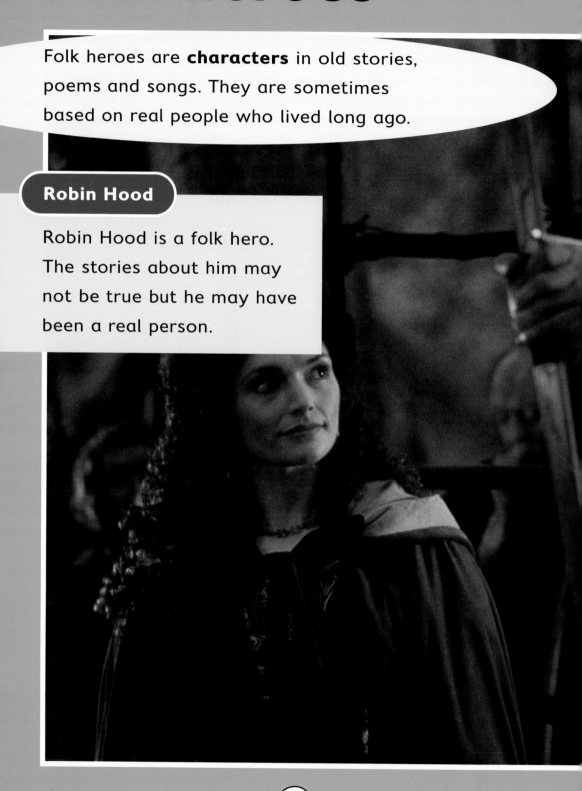

Robin Hood is an **outlaw**. He lives in the forest with his gang.

He kills the king's deer and robs rich people. But he is a hero because he helps the poor.

Zero to Hero (Part two)

Mrs Wilson yells at us and she blames us for everything too.

She blamed us when her window got smashed.

Okay, that *was* us. But it was an accident!

She blamed us when her fence got broken.

Okay, that was us again. But it was an accident.

We even said we were sorry.

She blamed us when there was graffiti on her garage door.

That *wasn't* us. We don't do graffiti.

But Mrs Wilson told the police we did it.

The police came to our house and we told them we didn't do it.

Then the police looked at the tag on the graffiti. They knew we didn't do it, too.

Continued on page 36

Super villains

Super villains are often the enemies of superheroes. Some super villains have super powers.

The Green Goblin

The Green Goblin is a comic-book super villain. He wants to kill Spiderman.

He wears a goblin costume and travels on a gadget called a goblin glider.

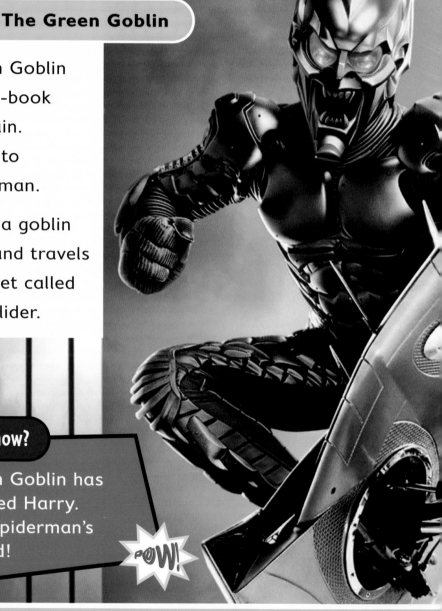

Did you know?

The Green Goblin has a son called Harry. Harry is Spiderman's best friend!

POW!

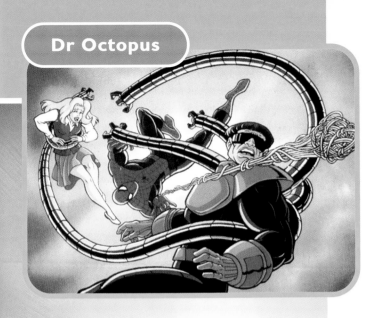

Dr Octopus

Dr Octopus is another of Spiderman's enemies.

He has four **titanium** tentacles on his body. He uses them to run and climb.

Villain fact!

Dr Octopus controls his tentacles with the power of his mind.

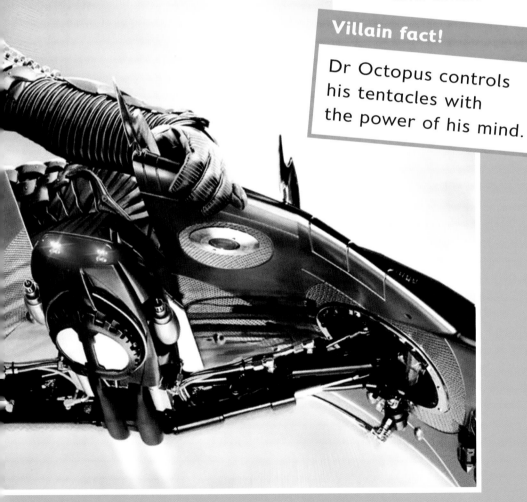

Villains in books

Orcs

Orcs work for the villains
Saruman and Sauron in
the 'Lord of the Rings' books.
Orcs are short, ugly creatures
that eat human flesh!

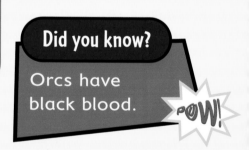

Did you know?

Orcs have
black blood.

POW!

Big, tall Orcs are called Uruks.
They are a cross between Orcs and Men.

Dracula

Dracula is a **vampire**. In the book 'Dracula', he comes to England and attacks several women.

A man called Van Helsing hunts down Dracula. He stabs Dracula through the heart and Dracula turns to dust.

Vampire fact!

Vampires have no reflection or shadow.

Villains in films

In films, the villain is often called the 'baddie'.

James Bond meets many villains.

Odd Job

Odd Job works for Goldfinger.
He uses his hat to kill people.

Jaws

Jaws is tall and strong with big
metal teeth. He's in two Bond
films but he says only four words.

Blofeld

Blofeld and his cat are in six
Bond films. Blofeld is killed after
he kills James Bond's wife.
His cat survives.

Darth Vader is the best-known villain in the 'Star Wars' films. But he is not a villain in all the films.

Darth Vader

At first, Darth Vader is a Jedi Knight and a hero. Then he moves to the Dark Side and becomes a villain.

Before he dies, he turns his back on the Dark Side to save his son's life.

Real-life villains

Jack the Ripper

Jack the Ripper was a famous
murderer in Victorian times.
No one really knows who he
was or how many people he killed.

He may have killed three women
or he may have killed up to 11.

No one really knows because Jack
the Ripper was never caught.

Dr Crippen

In 1910, Dr Crippen killed his wife. He cut up her body and threw her head into the sea. He burnt her bones. Then he hid the rest of her body in the cellar.

Crippen told the police that his wife had gone away. But the police dug up the cellar and found her body. Crippen was hanged.

Did you know?

The UK doesn't hang people for crimes any more. The last hanging was in 1964.

Al Capone

Al Capone was a killer and a gangster. He lived in the United States in the 1900s. For years, the police couldn't catch him.

He was finally caught in 1932 but only for not paying his taxes!

Robert De Niro played Al Capone in the film 'The Untouchables'.

Did you know?

Al Capone's nickname was Scarface.

The Great Train Robbers

The Great Train Robbers stole money from a post-office train.

They took £2.6 million. The police caught the gang by finding their fingerprints on a Monopoly board at their hideout.

The gang had been playing Monopoly with real money. They each went to prison for 20 or 30 years.

The Great Train Robbers' actual Monopoly board and money

Zero to Hero (Part three)

We were very angry with Mrs Wilson.

She had blamed us for something we
didn't do.

The police told her we didn't do the graffiti.
But she didn't even say sorry to us!

The next day, Mrs Wilson's tyres were flat.
She blamed us, of course.

That afternoon, we rode our skateboards to the park.

We passed the pond. A woman was sitting on a bench reading a newspaper.

Her little boy was pushing the baby in a buggy. He was pushing the buggy up and down the path.

He saw us skating towards him. He pushed the buggy off the path to make way for us.

Continued on the next page

Zero to Hero (Part four)

But the buggy was on a hill. It started to roll down the hill. It started to roll towards the pond.

Russ yelled at me, "Quick, grab the buggy!"

The woman looked up from her newspaper and screamed.

It was Mrs Wilson.

Russ and I skated like mad. Just as the buggy got to the pond, we grabbed it.

Our boards shot into the pond and sank in the deep mud.

But the baby was safe!

Mrs Wilson was crying. She hugged her little boy. She hugged the baby. She even hugged us.

She told everyone we were her heroes. She even bought us new skateboards.

So we didn't tell her we were the ones who had let down her tyres!

Pirates

A pirate is a villain who attacks and robs ships.

There are still pirates today. There were more than 170 pirate attacks in 2006.

Blackbeard

Blackbeard was a real-life pirate who lived in the 1700s. He had a long, black beard and pigtails.

Blackbeard carried six pistols, two swords and lots of knives. People were terrified of him.

Pirate fact!

After Blackbeard was killed, his head was cut off.

Captain Jack Sparrow is a **fictional** pirate.

In the 'Pirates of the Caribbean' films, Jack is a villain.
He lies and cheats and steals ships and treasure.

Jack Sparrow

But Jack is not all bad.
He is a funny and
likeable villain.

Did you know?

The 'Pirates of
the Caribbean' films
were named after a
Disney park ride.

POW!

Folk villains

Folk villains are **characters** in old stories, poems and songs. They are sometimes based on real people who lived long ago.

Sweeney Todd is a folk villain. People have told stories about Sweeney Todd since Victorian times.

Sweeney Todd

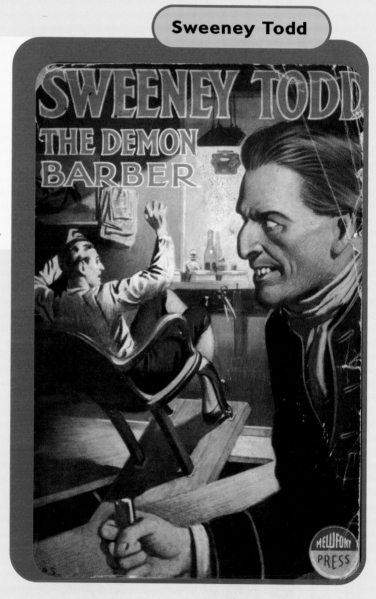

Some people think there was a real
Sweeney Todd but it isn't likely.

In the stories, Sweeney Todd is
a barber in London.

He kills lots of his customers.
He cuts their throats and tips
the bodies into his cellar.

The woman next door makes
meat pies from the bodies!

Quiz

1 What is Spiderman's real name?

2 Who does Alex Rider work for?

3 Who used a jet pack to escape from his enemies?

4 Who saved over 1,000 factory workers?

5 Why was Johnson Beharry given a Victoria Cross?

6 Who do the Orcs work for?

7 How did Dracula die?

8 Which Bond villain has big metal teeth?

9 Where did the police find parts of
   Mrs Crippen's body?

10 What do you call a villain who robs ships?

Glossary of terms

ambush	A surprise attack.
Antarctic	The land around the South Pole.
character	A person in a book, a play or a film.
diabetic	A person whose blood does not absorb sugar and starches properly.
fictional	Something that is made up or invented.
hunger strike	To protest by refusing to eat.
Nazi	A member of the German National Socialist party.
outlaw	A person who breaks the law.
science fiction	Stories set in an imagined world or involving imagined scientific discoveries such as time travel.
titanium	A strong, light metal.
vampire	A fictional creature that drinks blood to survive.
Warrior	A type of armoured vehicle used by the British Army.

More resources

Books

**Pirates of the Caribbean –
The Visual Guide**
Richard Platt
Published by Dorling Kindersley (ISBN: 978-1-40531-432-9)
Lots of photos from the films.

**Stormbreaker –
The Graphic Novel**
A Horowitz
Published by Walker (ISBN: 1844281116)
A comic book version of the first Alex Rider book.

You can listen to the Alex Rider books on audio CD.

Magazines

Doctor Who Adventures
BBC Magazines
Comic strip stories, competitions, puzzles and news

DVDS

Batman Begins
DVD Cert 12

Schindler's List
DVD Cert 15
How Schindler saved his workers from the Nazis.

Spiderman 1 and 2
DVD Cert PG

The Untouchables
DVD Cert 15
How Al Capone was eventually sent to prison.

Websites

www.alexrider.com
All you need to know about Alex and his missions.

www.bbc.co.uk/science/hottopics/jamesbond/
Lots of information and facts. It's good on Bond
gadgets and villains.

Answers

1 Peter Parker

2 MI6

3 James Bond

4 Oscar Schindler

5 Even though he was badly injured, he twice saved the lives of the soldiers with him in Iraq

6 The Orcs work for the villains Saruman and Sauron.

7 Van Helsing stabbed Dracula through the heart.

8 Jaws

9 The police found parts of Mrs Crippen's body in the cellar.

10 A pirate

Index